summersdale

PIMP YOUR PET
Copyright © Summersdale Publishers Ltd 2008
Written by A. J. Martin and designed by Rob Smith

Summersdale Publishers Ltd
46 West Street
Chichester
West Sussex
PO19 1RP
UK

www.summersdale.com

Printed and bound in Italy by Grafica Veneta S.p.A.

All images © Shutterstock

ISBN: 978-1-84024-713-8

'To err is human, to pimp is mighty fine'

INTRODUCTION

We humans are spoiled for choice: what shoes to wear, whether to get a tattoo or pierce our belly-button, whether to pick our nose in public or to save it for a quiet moment to ourselves, whether to don a suit and go corporate or squeeze on a 40 denier stocking over our noggin and rob a bank…

No such choices for the loyal moggy or pampered pooch in our lives – they're stuck wearing their birthday suits and doing the same things day in, day out. Until now.

Pimp Your Pet is the answer to your furry friends' prayers – now they can dress up and live out their fantasies to their hearts' content!

WARNING: do not use glue on your pet!

MOGGY GOLIGHTLY

long cigarette holder

diamond choker

tiara

beauty spot

big eyelashes

small guitar

APOCALYPSE CHOW

army beret

 **ammunition belt**

helicopter

 **sunglasses**

GANGSTA HAMSTER

ring

gold tooth

bling chain

sunnies

pumps

diamond stud

trilby

DRUG TSAR BUDGERIGAR

fedora hat

large suspicious roll-up

big 'tache

poncho

THE HOOF

large curly bouffant

big white teeth

chest wig

black car

leather jacket

GUANTANAMO GOLDFISH

black hood

razor wire

isolation tank

ball and chain

SNAKE HIPS

quiff

Vegas sunnies

glittery outfit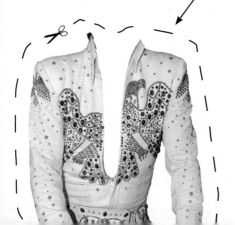

mic stand

CLOSE ENCOUNTERS OF THE FURRED KIND

alien helmet

spaceship

spaceship ramp

green dye

CHE CHIHUAHUA

cigar

Che mask

beret

RESERVOIR FROGS

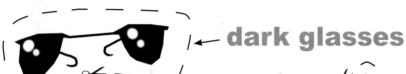

dark glasses

blood-splattered
suit and tie

gun

DOCTOR MOO

edgy new haircut

sonic screwdriver

big scarf

glasses

guitar

curly hair

vinyl

ZORBA THE SQUEAK

hat with tassel

shoes with
pom-poms

blue skirt

HUSTLIN' HOOF

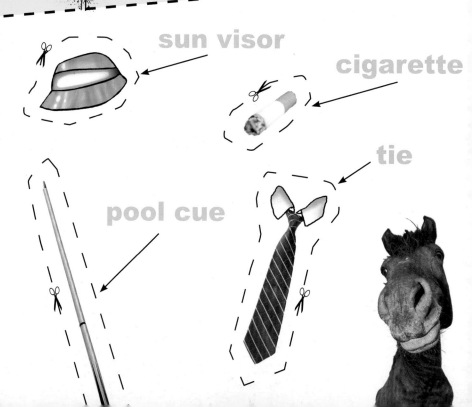

sun visor

cigarette

tie

pool cue

mad eyes

big jaunty
eyebrows

karate outfit

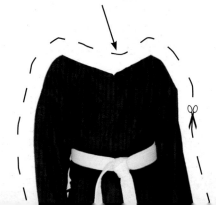

CHIN'ZILLA

tail

tooth extensions

scales

city in terror

CHAV CHICK

coin ring

hoop earrings

hooded sports top

tacky high heels

DICK TERRAPIN

old-fashioned pistol

mask

horse

swag bag

CHAINSAW CHILLA!

chainsaw

blood stains

mask

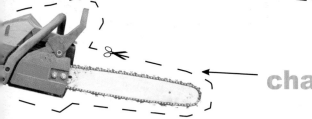

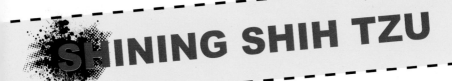

SHINING SHIH TZU

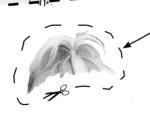

big sticky up hair

mad eyes

axe

door with a hole in

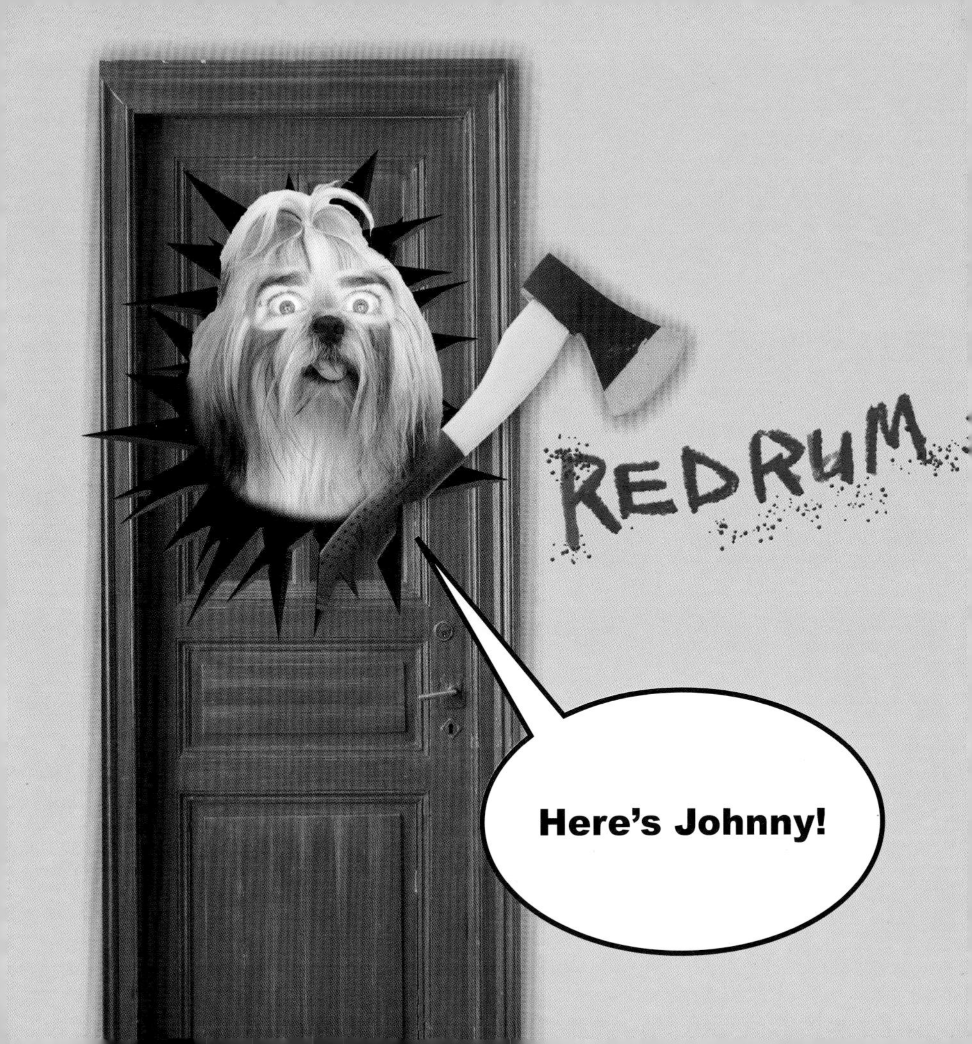
REDRUM
Here's Johnny!

MOUSEL MOUSEAU

stripy top

 **hat with flower**

black ballet shoes

 **white gloves**

HAWAII FI-DO

cap

Hawaiian shirt

police badge

speed boat

HAMBO

machine gun →

 ← **face camo**

headband →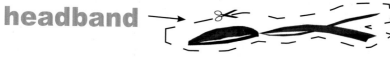

sweaty black vest

TREKKIE TERRIER

badge

pointy ears

slanted eyebrows

strange haircut

JACK SPARRA'

tricorn hat

sword

funky dreads with braids

beard and moustache →

earring

magic compass

HAMMYBAL LECTER

 mask

nice Chianti

straitjacket

BIG BUN

double-decker bus

black cab

clock tower

DON CURLY PONY

sneer

moustache

bow tie

rose

captain's hat

surveillance deck

$2.6 billion attack submarine

FRED HAMSTAIRE

top hat

silver-tipped cane

white bow tie

tap shoes

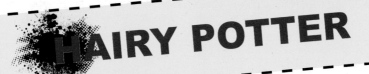

HAIRY POTTER

broomstick

 **round spectacles**

stripy scarf

wand

ALPACA-CHINO

eighties haircut

angry sneer

big gun

blood-stained shirt

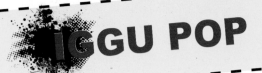
IGGU POP

rock star hair

tight leather pants

microphone

STICK-KNOT

tiny masks

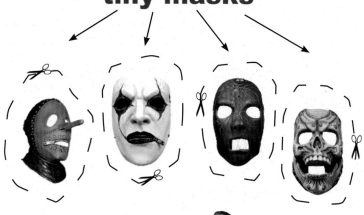

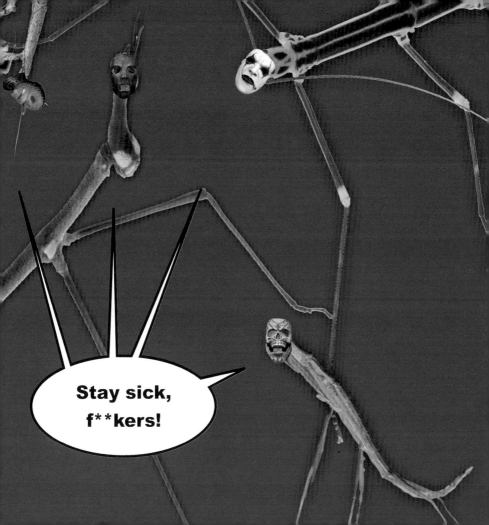

HELL'S ANGELFISH

skull necklace

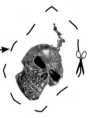

motorbike

crash helmet

JABBA THE MUTT

Jabba eyes

lizard tongue

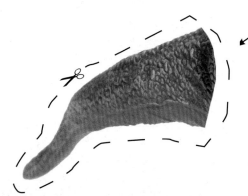

long tail

HENDRIX

headband

big afro

guitar

hippy scarf

wall of amps

big shoes →

← **small dresses**

pouty lips →

NEO NEWT

cool shades →

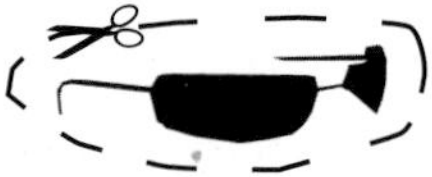

big billowing coat

red and
blue pills

mobile phone →

ball of string
(to suspend one's newt)

KARATE KID

rising sun headband

karate outfit

black belt

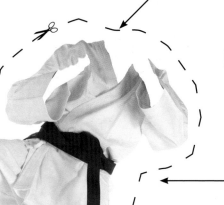

ACKNOWLEDGEMENTS

The authors would like to thank the Summersdale team for being great: Lucy, Ianthe, Jen, Gemma, Bert, Kirsty, Elly, Nicky, Dean and Alastair. Not forgetting Milla and Tom who helped with some of the captions.

Rob would like to give special thanks to the Magic Wand tool and the 165 little pairs of scissors in this book.

Pets with Tourette's

Mike Lepine & Mark Leigh

ISBN 13: 978-1-84024-610-0   Hardback   £5.99

Oh dear. It seems that our furry friends have been afflicted with a bad case of the swearing tic (not the wriggly kind you remove from your dog's back).

From foul-mouthed Fidos to fish that say 'f***!', *Pets with Tourette's* combines comical and cute photos with inappropriate captions to tickle the belly of animal lovers everywhere.

'... guaranteed to tickle anyone's sense of humour'
                                                        DAILY SPORT

'Book of the year!'   POPBITCH newsletter

'... will have you laughing for hours'   Borderslocal.co.uk

More Pets with Tourette's

Mike Lepine & Mark Leigh

ISBN 13: 978-1-84024-698-8   Hardback   £5.99

The swearing epidemic tightens its grip on the animal kingdom in this follow-up to the cult best-seller, *Pets with Tourette's*. Full to the brim with foul-mouthed pets, this hilarious collection of blaspheming bunnies and cussing kitties is the ultimate in unstoppable bad language.

Be warned: you might not be able to look your pet hamster in the face again...

www.summersdale.com